HOUSE A

HOUSE A

Jennifer S. Cheng

OMNIDAWN PUBLISHING
OAKLAND, CALIFORNIA
2016

Cover photograph by Mitsu Yoshikawa.
www.mitsuyoshikawa-image.com

Cover and interior text set in Optima LT Std and Adobe Garamond Pro

Cover and interior design by Gillian Olivia Blythe Hamel

Printed in the United States
by Books International, Dulles, Virginia
On 55# Glatfelter B19 Antique
Acid Free Archival Quality Recycled Paper

Library of Congress Cataloging-in-Publication Data

Names: Cheng, Jennifer S., 1983- author.
Title: House A / Jennifer S. Cheng.
Description: Oakland, California : Omnidawn Publishing, 2016.
Identifiers: LCCN 2016015123 | ISBN 9781632430236 (pbk. : alk.paper)
Classification: LCC PS3603.H4598 A6 2016 | DDC 811/.6--dc23
LC record available at https://lccn.loc.gov/2016015123

Published by Omnidawn Publishing, Oakland, California
www.omnidawn.com (510) 237-5472 (800) 792-4957
10 9 8 7 6 5 4 3 2 2
ISBN: 978-1-63243-023-6

For my parents, James and Li-Ma Cheng, who gave me my cosmology of home.

Contents

In making for ourselves a place to live,
we first spread a parasol to throw a shadow on the earth,
and in the pale light of the shadow we put together a house.

—*J. Tanizaki,* In Praise of Shadows

*

Our house is our corner of the world.
...[I]t is our first universe, a real cosmos.

—*G. Bachelard,* Poetics of Space

LETTERS TO MAO

A house of dream-memory, that is lost in the shadow of a beyond...

—Bachelard

Dear Mao,

I want to describe for you the feeling of sleep, as described by neuropsychologist Giulio Tononi, who uses words like *oscillations* and *waves*, while his patient is noted to gather the phrase *the sea moving a boat*. Elsewhere are words like *sleepwalking* and *daydreaming*, so I can only conclude that sleep is a boundary whose line is slowly eroding. Sleep, like childhood, is more of a sense than an experience we can articulate from beginning to end. As a child in Texas bathed in sun, I often fell asleep in the car, even in daytime, and my father would carry me into the house with my head pressed against his shoulder. If my mother, who is much smaller, was the driver, she would crack open a window on warm afternoons, and I would later wake to the pleasure of utter silence and aloneness, the sun across my face. I want to emphasize to you that both responses were acts of love, and if by chance an airplane overhead excavated an echo in the sky, then I knew that I was cradled in its sound. Inside our home of secret languages, my mother boiled up a pot of salty rice porridge and my father watched our neighbors like a devout mockingbird: straw doormats, pine wreaths in the winter. So I want you to know that if sleep is an ocean, then it is because we are migrants inwardly sighing along to its many oscillations, unintimidated by factual distances but awash in the knowledge of three: body, bodying, embodied. And if water is a metaphor, then it is because water fills up a room, slow-moving, blurry, immersive but obscured. Strangely enough, it was not my father but my mother who gave us history lessons steeped in a pale, languorous liquid: we sleep where our home is, and we build a home where we sleep.

Dear Mao,

For mine was a childhood of mooring and unmooring as I lay waiting for sleep to come in a dusty bed with a pale blue coverlet. Like many small children, I often woke in the middle of the night and moved around in my sheets as if loosening angels in the snow, a half-open fan. Sometimes these half-asleep movements lead me beyond the boundaries of my bed, to pick up my little pillow from the shadow of the floor, or to the edge of the living room where the noise of the television had diffused my dreams. It was here one night I found the blurry shape of my father, a comforting figure at odds with the noise; he picked me up gently, murmuring, and entrusted me back into the softened mound. I tell you this now because I want you to understand that my father was the kind of father who reimagined mythical stories as we lay in my parents' bed at night, a ritual that was less the antics of our beloved *Sun Wu Kong* and more the rising and falling of my father's voice wrapped around such images and sounds. *Boundary, binding, bond.* It is important for you to understand that never once did I long for a different life, which is not to say I never longed for home. I mean this, of course, in an untethered, abstract, and metaphysical sense: for although as a child I was often homesick—at school, at the neighbor's house, anywhere unfamiliar or foreign—I also at times felt an inexplicable longing while inside my own house.

Dear Mao,

I want to describe for you the migration pattern of birds, which has nothing to do with sleep but which I nonetheless find beautiful. When insects sleep, they are wakened only by poetic forces, like the heat of the sun or the darkness of night. The most beautiful of flying insects huddle together in sleep, but little is known about the slumbering habits of migratory birds. Birds, as far as I know, do not fear being shot down from the sky, though fear is a common warning sign for flight. Some birds, feeling their bones weighed down by air, migrate not by sky but by swimming, their wings waving down the sea as if buoyed by its girth. Other birds are wanderers, their migratory curvatures charted like flowering seeds across the globe. Here on the earth where bones are buried, the question remains: if the birds of history alight by a ritual of body and landscape, do they make the return out of longing, out of heartache? For it is the anthropologist who traces the longing for home between personal biography and the biography of the collective, a map that ends beyond locatable distances into mythical terrains, imaginary homelands. We do this: listen to the body, gauge its violence, take flight.

Dear Mao,

At the end of the day, longing for home is a narrative we are both familiar with, beginning first with a poem about the moon. If my parents never pointed at a map, it was because we already had an earthy-colored globe that I spun round and round until the smell of rice porridge drew me near the kitchen. So that ours was always a story of leaving and never an anchoring of place.

Dear Mao,

When my mother first told me the folktale of the woman in the moon, I thought it was a story of the evils of man. You will remember how the archer aimed upward and shot down the nine suns, saving the earth from scorching heat, but then out of conceit and possibly psychosis, he wanted to shoot the final tenth sun, just so he could watch his fire bleed across the sky. In school we learned the mythology of Zeus, and all I could think was, what kind of people imagine for themselves a god who punishes the innocent and ravages women? Narrative, as we know, is an essential marker in child development. A child achieves story grammar around the same age that she learns to recognize her body as her own; before that, people are an interconnected sea. We all long for narrative. Mine begins with water or sleep, or the feeling of my parents moving about the house on summer afternoons. In the summers, they would open the windows of our Texas house and let in the smell of warm grass, and as I wandered into the kitchen where Shanghainese opera frolicked through the static of our old radio, I often heard rather than saw my mother walking around barefoot, mixing sticky ground meat with scallions and cooking wine. This can be a kind of narrative: scents of backyard plants, the acoustics of kitchen linoleum, cold *lu dou tang* to follow up our lunches. What if I were to name my children after heroic figures of ancient Greece? Theseus, Achilles, Hector.

Dear Mao,

Inhabited surface, like the wooden grain surrounding an embedded nail. It was there in our second home that my father built the table where we ate our meals. In other words, we gathered around the table my father built. And it was there in the summers of tornado season that we huddled in the bathtub while my father stood watch at the living room window, looking for tunneling cones or roofs detaching.

Dear Mao,

Later in the summer when my father found a wasp nest clinging to the cabinet, it was he who instructed me to go into my bedroom and shut the door. Our things were packed in boxes, the carpet mottled with pockmarks, and I knew it was the front door constantly open all day that had given up our house.

Dear Mao,

We could call this *How to Build an American Home*, or *History Lessons*, or even *Dislocated Objects* (misplaced nostalgia, broken cotton slippers, a shelf of souvenir dolls in slow wave sleep). Or: I found a vast stamp collection and various paraphernalia on the top shelf of my father's cabinet in Texas, your face was plastered on its pages. I was standing tippy-toe on the counter, and my fingers got printed in dust. I suppose I could say, *history is personal* or *history of others*, but we both know how to substitute "as" for those two-letter verbs and prepositions. Dear Mao: 800,000 soldiers, 30 million peasants, parades of old litter and scrap metal squads. Dear Mao: Waterbugs flee. Seabirds flee. They would like to make it clear: they love their kelp, their underwater tempo, but let us have ourselves a parade of sea-wings. Dear Mao: A double-ended kaleidoscope. For we hate the evils of men, yet we will measure the circular path of the moon, we will wade through marshes in our rubber boots, we will stoop and pretend tiny plants or pools of stars are forests within which we begin construction, beginning with this creaky wooden frame. Dear Mao: When I was a child I wanted to wrap my mother's ferns and creamy violets in cozy sweaters, as this was the meaning of "potholders" I had internalized for myself. The coffee table was made of glass so I could see the carpet underneath, and it should come as no surprise that in the late afternoon, the light through the blinds cast a mesmerizing pattern of slanted stripes.

Dear Mao,

For one day I shall have the ability to convey the feeling of sleep, which is a feeling of dreams, stories, nightmares, and sometimes absolutely nothing. If sleep were a language, it would not sound like nothing but would instead materialize both longing and distance, history and myth. What I learned from my parents was the feeling of water, where all knowledge comes not in stories but in the tone of one's childhood, or the mood of a Saturday afternoon, or the sound of something boiling over when one is not looking. On the porch of our Texas house, I noticed that the summer evenings were quiet with the sound of large insects and crickets, which also sang longingly under my bed whenever I opportuned to wake in the middle of the night. The language of our home was similar to yours, though smoother like glass, and easier to tuck away. It is important to note that before language, children experience memories as image and sound, which is to say they experience them as poetry.

Dear Mao,

I hope you understand that what I am doing is trying to give you a history of water, which, like memory and sleep, is fluid and wafting in refracted light. *History as water*, so that I am giving you something that spreads.

Dear Mao,

In other words, sleep itself is porous. I know this is true because in the summers of my childhood I spent the occasional afternoon following my brother around while his neighborhood friend made up lies about his hallway closet as if it were some kind of wormhole, though this is an astronomical concept I would not learn till years later. My brother was offended by these lies, but I now know that the final stage of narrative language in childhood development is fiction, which is just another word for mythology. What right do we have to believe in history or homeland? Like the coastline of certain islands, these things change shape every so often and in gradual increments. I choose instead to believe in the rhythm of my father gathering his briefcase and shedding his slippers, or the familiar shape of my mother's hair, which began as short and sleek and grew in volume and curl until it was something ferocious like a bird's nest.

Dear Mao,

And how relieved I was no longer to be embarrassed by my mother's voice but to feel her broken sounds again as intimacy, as home. In this way childhood and adulthood came full circle, for it was in between the penance of adulthood and the poetry of a child that I stopped noticing whether the living room curtain was bringing in woolly light or a milder speckling. My siblings and I negotiated the front door with our comings and goings, but my mother never once complained about the infiltration. To be sure, she rarely spoke of her history or mine; instead between the light of holier days and birthday cakes with our names spelled out in fruit, I somewhere heard fragments like hand shadows that cannot be pinpointed; so it was that I absorbed your biggest sins.

Dear Mao,

For if the world, drowsy, were to be washed in a sheen, perhaps we would all have some intuitive knowledge of the immigrant body. And we do, at times: conscious of the ins and outs of how history holds us, or the ways we negotiate the space outside our bodies, noticing where and how we do not cohere. Stitched across my sleeping bag in thin silver lines is a contour map which resembles the ocean's own migratory movements, or the spreading of constellations across a dark chart. I like to lie in it and pretend it is enveloping me.

Dear Mao,

I am thinking of what it would mean for you to know the span of the coastline here on the Western edge, where I have migrated after thunderstorms and tree blossoms of varying terrains: winters of New England lawns, fields of Midwestern estrangement, Southwestern skies that never end. Some nights I dream of subtropical trees and their serpentine branches, but more and more my days are filled with escarpment and carapace scattered across the beach. The shells are emptied, abandoned; they are waiting for history to declare them whole. If ever my childhood were to belong to water, it would have been the years on a little island in the southern seas of your underbelly, where sleepy hillsides were always drenched in rain, and the childhood of my father was always bending around the next curve. *Landscape of embodied history*, and I am left wondering about the hidden roots of a banyan tree.

Dear Mao,

How, on the eve of the autumn moon, one of our paper lanterns caught fire. My sister and I were frightened, but my cousin stomped over it, leaving large curly ashes on the red-and-gray tiles. When it was over, we looked at each other and laughed. My sister and I ran through the evening warmth to the playground and swung on a rubber tire in circles as the crickets and insects trilled tirelessly.

Dear Mao,

For I know how a landscape can cradle a person home. If I could miscarry you all the way to the ocean. If I could, instead, pretend you were once a house made dirty by the fog. Inside an unfamiliar room, I inspect the dust and corners, behind the furniture, inside the tub. I look for ways in which to let the sunlight in and a place to hang papery birds. How to measure my body home, which is to say, how many names can you give to an immigrant's geography? *Delta Court, Tai Tam, Outer Sunset*; finally, a dream to reach the edge of the sea, where house inhabits multifaceted directions and hangs like a jar catching wind and grit in its mouth.

Dear Mao,

If I could, I would record for you the movement of the body in sleep, the way one shifts and gestures without even knowing it, how a cheek can quickly turn against a pillow, how a leg can sweep across the sheet. I never know what tiny lives are lost to me before I wake. These days I rise in the morning to either steamy hills or salty winds, both of which feel like deep breaths, but still I wonder how cold a lungful feels, if it strikes against the ribcage in an indescribable manner, if the body in other landscapes holds its seawater. For to say we have forgotten is to assume we once fully knew, but I have never known anything except white noise and the sound of traffic from very far away: it is like small animals gravitating in water. At the bottom of the ocean is a kind of creature that swims by opening and closing its outer shell like a mouth, as if propelled by soundless utterances. And what lessons does a child learn, as she watches the movements of her parents preparing the house in the mornings? The lights and shadows of their interactions were everywhere. In school we heard the narratives of Columbus and Pearl Harbor, and in college the professor gave lectures on Marxism, but whenever this happened, all I could think of was the dark silhouette of my mother's hair and how my father taught me to listen to the inside of a seashell.

Dear Mao,

What, after all, does the body know? The wind-blown trees at the edge of the cliff are going to fall into the sea, so we must tie them down, attach them to buoys so they may float indeterminately.

Dear Mao,

In between the flowers spreading a pink blanket along the shores, I am the girl with debris stuck between two fingers, like syllables one might lean in to hear. I would say— Lost: my fingernail moon. Lost: the dark spot inside my mother's throat. Lost: house inside my seams.

Dear Mao,

Even the island is not really an island, but a collection plus a splinter. Mapmaking poets believed in the supremacy of geography to history, but to them I would say that the hills outside my eastern hemisphere window resembled the contours of the afternoons I spent feeling cocooned underneath the staircase, listening as my mother rummaged around the kitchen. Another way to say this is that the lilt of the landscape resembled the lilt of our language between these walls, a pattern of sounds ever represented by my mother's off-key lullabies. My mother, you understand, has never mapped anything, and often we find ourselves at a linguistic impasse. Yet once when I mentioned that I was often sad, she echoed this with the offering that she was often the same. It would not be, then, so far-fetched for me to say that even as a child, I knew how to long for home. Or: it was important for me to identify the other side of the globe as if it were mountains cradling my body. The island wasn't even yours.

Dear Mao,
Architectural palimpsest: a layer of skin I am inclined to peel.

Dear Mao,
My small mouth haunting the air.

Dear Mao,

How it was like this: the layout of the room: the air between us: evaporations and condensations of their morning rhythms spinning the room in which we slowed. How I want you to also know:

Dear Mao,

If I stare at the corner of the ceiling long enough, if a shape appears as large as an insect, as bent as my father's father's body, if its brief semblance of life displaces my breath, an urgency asleep in my veins, if sleep is something that pulls one under—

Dear Mao,
Such residue, the way a ghost becomes a blueprint. *Houseprint: house-pressed:*

Dear Mao,
Phantom limb.

Dear Mao,
We are all in aberrant atmospheres, hearing the dissonant tonal drifts blaring in our ears. We are all on hunt.

Dear Mao,

I want to describe for you the moment where we try to articulate what it is we are all longing for. My mother always told me that I need not divulge everything to a man, so these are things I shall divulge to you: My father's parents had an anger with history that I felt palpably even as a child; so it was with curiosity that I watched them return at the end of the summer to a home of mournful streets and a sky burnt with smoke. Here is another: Never mind the politics of water, distance for a child is a matter of fact. I saw my grandparents for a few weeks and then I didn't. I played in the shadow of rainy green hills and then I didn't. As an adult, distance feels like nostalgia. In the summer whenever we visited my maternal grandfather in Chicago, my mother and sister and I used to sleep on a mattress on the floor where the carpet smelled of orange peels and dried plums. We did not speak much, and most afternoons were spent walking to the public library, where afterward we lingered by the swings just as the air was beginning to smell of shadows. My father's parents were much farther away. Travelers, migrants, interlopers: these are sounds that preoccupy me in a way I do not know how to explain. It has to do with the ocean, which is 361 million square kilometers that boat dwellers navigated using the night sky as a map. Later on in school, I learned that spaces are divided into boundaries and shapes, and each of these shapes has a name.

Dear Mao,

To say your name plainly, as if you were a man of History I knew so well. My uncle as a twenty-year-old in prison, whispering, only it wasn't a whisper but a drunken fury, *They're trading children, do you understand? Everyone is starving.* I have no way of knowing if what he said is true, so why should history be so unreliable was what I asked myself. You in your stone peasant house by the wet fields. You attending primary school with the other village children. You running away at age eleven, believing the next town over was only footsteps away. You were dust in my house. A shadow underneath the floorboards.

Dear Mao,

I sleep lightly, like a long-legged insect skating atop the surface of a midland lake, but my mother is such a deep sleeper that when the Taiwan storms flooded her adolescent home, the water level had already washed upward of the table legs by the time she made her way out the door. She, like the others of her town, waded her way to the convent, where the nuns were handing out blankets, ready to host the masses in the only two-story building around for miles. What she will one day describe to me: the feeling of the water against her bare shins.

Dear Mao,

For we each live within our own language, some more literally than others, and mine is fractured into categories of intimate or functional, hard-pressed or textured, but never something without knots and gaps. If I could take a shadow and sew it to another until it formed a roof above my head. My brother napping on the couch in his winter jacket, I in the next room, murmuring imaginary happenings to myself as the angle of the sun caught the ascending dust. Outside, my father put up wooden beams around our plants, sanding the logs until they made a satisfying sound against the rubber of my shoe.

Dear Mao,

In stories we kept reading, wandering was a punishment, and we were instructed to pity the immigrant, the foreigner, the stranger. But what if the absence of a point of reference is not something to be lamented but a structural foundation on which to build a house we fill with water? Yes, this is my family name. Yes, there is a haze between the child of the West and the child who identifies with the sea.

Dear Mao,

When all I wanted was to stitch my languages together, even if with an ever escaping thread. For the tethering and untethering of boats has more to do with the night sky than the width of the strings we use.

Dear Mao,

Behind the fog, the lake is like a well-worn sheet gathered at the edges. What does it mean, my father as a child believing he would have to lie his body still at the bottom of a boat? Dear Mao: I used to be the kind of person who accepts things as they are: ciphers hidden in the lotus cakes, lanterns set to sea in order to lure the body home, rice bundles to keep the fish from eating holes in a drowned body's limbs. Our home in the south of the island slept between the ocean on one side, and on the other large dark hills, so I could always know what it was to be at the same time cocooned and ready to arch a distance. How I would brush my teeth in the darkness, afraid of the shadow at the window but comforted by the slopes I knew were lurking behind. Dear Mao: I never wanted my mother's body too far from my own.

Dear Mao,

If a sleeping bird were to dream, would it dream of icebergs, rocky cliffs, humid ponds? Or would it recall the feeling of winter settling in its tiny bones, reminding it just how wide the sky is across? For I can assemble a list of the ways we build—ranch-style house, colonial house, brick house, wooden gray slats—but we will never remember exactly how we began. *Estrangement from what?* is the question you will never answer. Standing there on a dirt path heading toward the waves, a sudden rush of birds from the bushes might sound like mottled thunder. *Dear Immigrant,* the anthropologist begins. As if this were a language where I am falling, where I am always falling asleep.

Dear Mao,

In the water of my house that sleeps, the sleeping house, the house of water. In the loosening of my childhood at sea, we imagine a map of imaginary seams to bind up the blue, the sea, as if it were a sleeping bag, a blue cocoon. Imaginary maps to represent a house: boat house, house on stilts, house ready to be pulled into the wind. House for the sleeping child, house rebuilt. Tidewater represents a yearning. In the sleeping house of intimate objects: ceramic horses; wooden baskets; stone abacus; corduroy yellow cushions; shiny ornamental ashtray. There is the water of my body navigating these landscapes, there is the extension of the body that is taking them in. Something is learned, something is enacted. In the arrangement of movement within sacred space—walls, weather, inscription. In the *archaeology of ritualized movement*, in the study of architectural forms: the anthropologist takes into account geography and staging, and finds in its spatial journey, its journey of sleep, a reconstruction of cosmology.

Dear Mao,

I want to describe for you the watery life of home, and by that I do not mean the ambiguity of homeland. For homeland is something embalmed in someone else's memory, or it is a symbol, both close to the heart and a stranger you reach for in the middle of the night. Symbols, as we know, can represent good or evil, and when my parents gave me their history lessons, they were always intimate, a personal language of the body, so I knew that facts and tenderness weren't separate things but came mixed together, like a glass of cloudy lemon-tea. Children tell their own histories, and so it is with this in mind that I tell you this story: When I was a child and living across the sea, my family traveled northward one summer to an unnamed place and stood staring at a portrait of a man. I cannot recall the expression on the faces of my parents, and I do not remember how long we lingered.

HOUSE A; GEOMETRY B

...to chart a new continent...this cracked-ceiling world...

—*Bachelard*

A

house: a building for human habitation;
a household.

house: any of the numbered divisions of
the celestial sphere.

B

geometry: concerning properties and
relationships: points, lines, surfaces,
solids, and higher dimensional
structures.

geometry: the shape and relative
arrangement of the parts of something.

a frame shaped; a house built around
such a [limbed] frame.

C

secret collection of A-frame houses:
photographs, images, illustrations.
variations, meaning *an angular
difference between true north at a
particular place*, or *a version of a theme,
modified in melody.*

secret accumulation of geometries:
gridded shapes, art installations,
platonic solids, old-fashioned diagrams.
"here we participate in the carpenter's
solid geometry," he said of the house.

iterations in offbeat measures, between
endpoints: the sun at opposite horizons.
rooms in a house of seamed structure,
unseaming an undetermined space.

(an immigrant dreams in unseen
amplitude: the distance at rising or
setting.)

repetitions, recurrences, retellings. i
keep them inside recycled jars: acorn,
paper star, tiny pinecone.

"a house constitutes a body of images."

D

a dream is slightly off-center if this rock
is where we place our heel to pivot. in
sleep, a dream spreads until it is a sea of
points and none of reference.

if we could construct, say, a physical
manifestation of an interior state.

where in the space, we take these angles,
fill it with air, and watch it hang from
the ceiling.

bird. shell. dry hibiscus.

let us pretend it is a loose-limbed
structure rather than something with a
surface no shadow can touch.

enumerated imprecision, like counting
the way an echo divides into lights and
breaks.

for the house is physically inscribed on
our bodies; a *diagram of the functions of
inhabiting* that house.

to map, to constellate, to excavate. a
blueprint for this mythos.

a house is a map we unfold carefully, lest
our breath is caught in the center ridge.

E

we build a house to locate ourselves; a
body lay in the house, a body lay slant in
the house.

say the word *nest* and they thought i
meant *child*.

inside the house, i look for smaller
houses.

structural beams of the kitchen table,
canopy of wounded quilts. jar for the
shell, jar for the birds, jar for the dry
hibiscus.

anthropology of house: *a* is for the space
between two slopes. the [weathering] of
the roof against outside [weather].

angle is the particular incline to reflect a
particular view. as in: here is the
baseline, here is the position along
which you travel.

weather: the shape of the atmosphere.
the side from which the wind is
blowing.

extracts: house, body, architecture.

F

"not in the thing itself but in the patterns of shadows": an after-effect that splinters over everything.

we moved upward inside the observatory shaped like a lighthouse, in order to peer through a telescope at blurred light.

G

to unfurl the body like breathing across a weathered dandelion: a poetics of [dislocation].

"a *no place*, a *nowhere*, an imaginary space longed for."

at any moment we may open a window. hear the ocean, let in the headlands, forgive the pine.

an unfinished place of historical and geographical boundaries.

H

he placed the household parts—beams, frames, boards—across a field in geometrical patterns.

she wove together long wooden strands into the shape of an oscillating womb.

if we were to say, the father is a *convex polyhedra*. or, he lay out the living room in *tetrahedron composed*.

archivist of preternatural composition. the house never failed to hold in light. as in: even when you closed your eyes, you could make out brightness.

take a shaded triangle, add thirteen more of four different shades, and you can construct a form with multiplied modes of seeing.

so we looked just above the horizon, no matter where the others were hanging their views.

I

say the word *shell* and they thought i meant *fear.*

say the word *seed* and they thought i meant *bury.*

say the word *distance,* and they thought i meant *absence.*

say the word *texture,* and they thought i meant *an external sensation.*

J

a series of connected points might look like a mountain range, just as a house might resemble the edge of my mother's skirt, the fold of the sky, an arch of crinkled trees from a distance.

imagine three layers in the crest of a
window as if it were a cross-sectioned
plane: dark sienna hill, bright blue sea,
cold eggshell sky. thicknesses of
specified materials. consistencies framed
inside a container.

or the early morning projecting
shadows of hanging things onto a
surface.

reverberations of form, texture,
directionality; or, tracing the negative
space as its own body of light.

K

let us make for ourselves a catalogue of
migratory shapes: the lady in the moon,
he, she, eucalyptus tree.

if we mimic their trajectories in dotted
lines, draw [constellations] into a kept
surface, embroider [vectors] onto the
walls of a room in which you are
contained.

if we suspend a weather system inside a
hallway, its longing the shape of the
smallest hour.

if we hear reflections of sound waves or
glimpse a secondary shadow.

dear house, dear ocean, dear triangle of
suspended light.

L

and the cardinal points of such a space?
we might say a heptagon is *water*, a
nonagon is *sleep*.

a body orbits; pathways between
furniture form a constellatory map.
corollary lines by which we hinge and
unhinge ourselves to corner lamplight,
flaxen wallpaper, a remembrance of
water pipes.

(to fixed horizons, to vanishing points,
to subtle shifts in wind direction.)

M

take the world's materials and make for
ourselves a space in which to keep a
weather eye.

think of, say, the frames of the windows
or the ritual of blinds and curtains.

a house from which we learn to
recognize atmospheric patterns.

cumulonimbus, cirrus, cirrostratus.

instead of pointing and naming, i would
look up and the space from which i
watched would earth its memory in
temperatures, filters, sequences.

arrangement of sunlight reflecting off
arrangement of furniture: a map that
sinks inside the body as the day wears
on.

N

for a ceiling is not white but casts an
array of varied shades, bands of light,
watery globules.

every sound of traffic beyond the
window is then accompanied by moving
blocks of geometric light that glide and
blink across the bare expanse.

lying on my back, i can be awash, noting
how an exterior affair of sound and
existence transforms into a mood of
interior shapes.

a house leaves many shadows.

O

"and when the seeping starts, the house
is already completed"

P

configuration, constellation.

*a poetics of hung laundry, mild-hearted
plants atop cold tile floors, her mother's
half-reflection in a morning window.*

weave together a contradiction of
silences and angles, grainy and soft: a
viewfinder we find necessary to
approximate the [margins].

itinerant shadows, shadow equations,
kinship of [nodes] denoting.

how, eventually, an atmosphere of triangles comes to resemble crinkled paper.

how, underneath a mesh skylight, the room becomes a woven nest.

textures and contours that reach for the body in context.

where *context* is rarely an empty structure but always a concavity of tonal notes, set to circuitous beats.

Q

instead of a house: the noise of a tunnel: or, vice versa.

an act of translation: building a house/structure to represent the tone/texture.

an immigrant is like this: *cirrus, circular, circulate.*

R

if i suspend an open polyhedron made of thin rods and string, hanging from a doorframe, each plane would be composed of various outlines of the room: rain-dotted pane, stripes of brittle wood, *willow herb* of the wall.

if i then suspend it in the park, on the street, against the city grid.

S

(if the distance he crossed were the
grout between ceramic tiles. if the
language she spoke was the clarity of the
air, the humidity reading of a room).

T

a poetics of distance, of [aberrant]
geometries: to rename the anchor, to
cast a pall over it.

"identify and measure the [acoustic
intervals] of global migration,
settlement, histories and
historiography"

in lieu of the weather ever-shifting, a
mother and father built up the frame,
measured out the circumferences of
worlds within.

we traveled through the living room in
dihedral angles and *spherical excess*.

the house seeps, the body mirrors.

its creases form an array of bright
intersections and radiating lines.

U.

not the lost house, not the forgotten
house, but the house of echoes.

the petals of their rustling in the
kitchen, in the slow garden: the veins of
their mild routines: a chart unnoticed,

an asterism unseen: how it stitched a wound for my body, and for none of the stones outside.

the way i wrapped her sound around my hand: a soft eave i could keep like folded cloth.

let us say the interaction of colorful spools threaded around the body, as it sat in the flooded dark or against the curve of her mother.

she arranged her body in *stratus nebulosus*.

helix of her ocean breath. axis of her non-evaporated sky.

V

the body of a house:

sleeping fossil

geometric shell

W

a window printed in dust and debris marks a meeting point of outside weathers, inside movements.

she cut a shape and called it *window*. he stitched a hinge and called it *door*.

the [condensation] of a house: a series of overlaying transparencies variantly grainy with collations and soot.

obscurity of the moon, likeness of the window, skin of the glass.

a might be the dimension of nightlight staining the body, encoding a pattern of angles and ghosts. *b* might be the straining of mid-afternoon silence.

X

suppose an attic is where the history of a past is stored away. in the absence of a partition, this house is everywhere the angle of that apex, spread as an umbrella, a roof in the truest sense.

let us define nostalgia, then, not as a remembrance but a feeling, *familial*, that is on a precipice, vulnerable to the winds, drifting and swelling for a nest.

i have roots that are most [secret], i am grown in the deep earth.

to chart a shadow is to draw a body closer to its longing. let us say a house's dislocation is located in the yearning of the blinds, horizontal intimacies strewn across the floor.

figure x is the angle at which the floorboards push back at the projection of windowlight.

Y

a might be her unlocated hum settling its sleep between the leaves of a dried-up cane plant.

b might be a [spectrogram] of their circulations, impressed upon this envelope of air.

Z

the body of articulation occurs through a house.

"possible [metrics]: contact zone, borderlands. language in construction of multiple histories."

let us iterate it until it is its own baseline. dislocation as house. longing as location. ·

HOW TO BUILD AN AMERICAN HOME

...We are going to build a house.

—*Bachelard*

How to Build an American Home

In order to travel from one house to another without touching the cracks,
a network of points and people must be absorbed. Intersecting routes of
familial intention and linguistic obligation: a prism-shaped notion
of belonging. On its surface, such criss-crossing could be seen as interference,
but I prefer an accident of geometry. Without such nodes, we are merely
dropped satellites blinking as the earth approaches midnight.

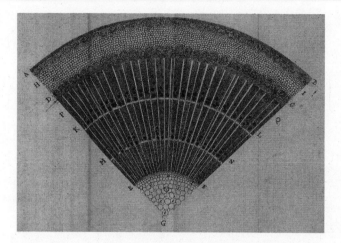

The first time I learned how we all inhabit an acoustic architecture of space,
it was sound traveling across a landscape, contouring objects, carving
between them, bringing forth a movement of bodies through space. You
could stand inside a metal sculpture of a whale, close your eyes; or you could
walk in an underground tunnel toward a concrete echo. The house is an
arrangement of objects with which we move through the world. We become
familiar with a system of echolocation. Children of immigrants
take their house wherever they go, its sounds patter and shake like a
drawerful of dishes, cups, spoons.

How to Build an American Home

In the intercession of all things waning, we will
remember each object represents a texture,

coexistence between one's body and an inhabited surface.

First is the wooden seat her father made so she could reach
the bathroom sink. On one side of the wood was a circular stain, a
birthmark that became her friend.

Second is the hum of the heat
lamp as he cuts her hair, little dark nestings around the tub. Wire tubes glow
red behind a cage; he cautions them away.

Third is a world embalmed in *field artefacts*. Her mother and father opening
doors, looking for something to hold the moon.

How to Build an American Home

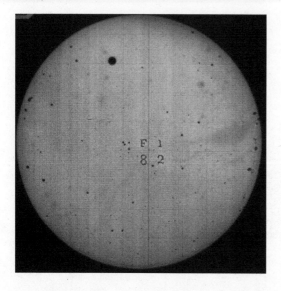

If the body is the source of all language,
                              semantic template,
        if our limbs, skin, organs enact meaning like a metaphor, before
        we are able to speak it;

                              we could for sure trace the square
of light projected from the window onto the wall;
                              you might believe me when I gesture
toward the edges in all their woolly glory

                                        or find in my throat
                a brown-winged insect,
                        transiting,
                for a shadow in which to meet.

How to Build an American Home

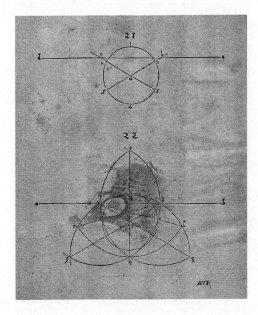

A house is a body; it is not permeable.

    Inside, we grow a forest of moon, marsh, bird. Outside, the world looms large and flat as a paper hole in the ceilingspace.

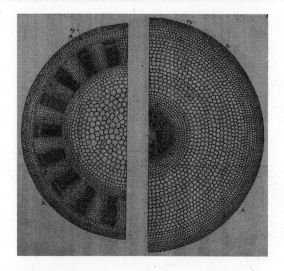

For example:
When a girl leaves to marry another, a process of mourning begins. Light hits the earth at an undigested angle, and we carry ourselves to the river.

On the third day, the couple will return to her home in homage: two steps forward, one step back. A slow process, emanating years, *anatomy of plant relations,* a leaf fallen and carried out by the tide.
She will hold heart in one hand.

How to Build an American Home

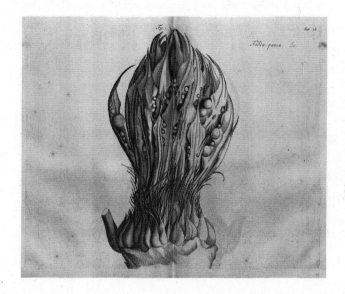

Or:
To keep the body sound,
sheathe the belly. Fortify water, shield bones and ginger in
measurements of roots,
   black wood ear, vinegar. Safe the *dragon eye.*

      Inside this margin
of water I watched it like a layer of tissue in which to stay
    warm. Inside a shell
  we are all: spilling, dissolved. Inside a blight, blur: all (un)
      known.

To say *home* is a *whole* that keeps us
apart from others;
a membrane cannot help insulating distance—

The house is a texture
we leave in our trails, a boundary laid to hold ourselves.
Close to the ground, I can hear
sky. Wrapped in the dirt, I can sense *wave*.
In the shadow we have splintered, the skin is a curve
only I can gather, the weave of the grain only I can bear.

How to Build an American Home

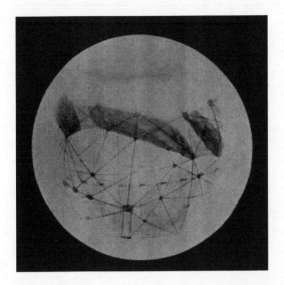

                                                            If this house could stand
on one edge and beckon to the rest of the darker waves, as if to say, *here.*
A house on the edge is a house ready to unseam itself against the contour of
things unseen.

                                    In the great wind of the ocean, this house might begin to
murmur and speak in all the unpredictable places: groans in the bathroom tile
cracks, creaks at the entryway shade. Heard from the other side, its noises
might carry particulates into inarticulable spaces.

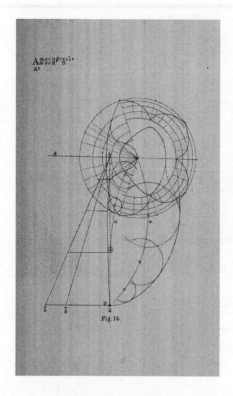

When I looked through a telescope of mirrors and windmills and
saw the Pleiades, a clear constellation, and the beehive cluster of several
bright dots—

Children of those who parachute in
go about their days collecting answers to questions not yet posed: *the creak
of a house breaking, a ritual of numbers, sound anatomy of her mother's call...*

How to Build an American Home

The father collected documents, ledgers, photographs. Newspaper clippings, cutout and creased, of either alphabet letters or intimate print.

On his first day in a new country, he walked from water to water, as if to test the boundaries. As if the daylight could be enough to gather oneself against such paper-thin sky.

How to Build an American Home

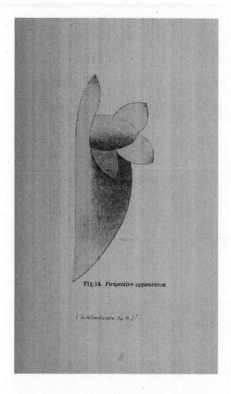

Fig.14. *Perspective appearance.*

{ To follow the after Fig 14. }

In this carton of tired bones, a storm grew inside me. *Save half
your belongings,* my father said. I hide
money around the house; my mother sends red envelopes
to carry every twelfth moon.

How to Build an American Home

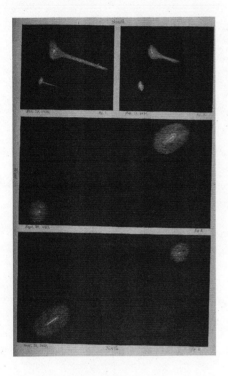

Embodied space:

If the body's orientation, inhabitation of a small or charged space
      structuration, saturation

                          is a record, document, map;

      Figures in the house circling like moths;
                her body crescented.

Her mother in the house is the house :
in the kitchen splitting roots : families split, bodies split, history split : sound
splitting : not a word, but a texture, terrain : not a speech, but a depth, density :
the structural foundation, the wall's stuffing : a fact of houses everywhere.

How to Build an American Home

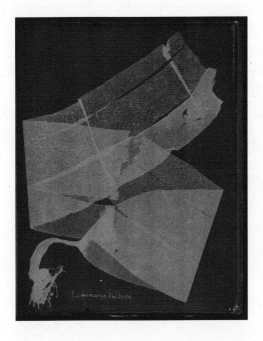

hart instead of *heart*; *cloth* instead of *clothes*
> *may be, air port*, a breath of air where there was none
>> *very beauty*
> *all your love to us*

I am look like from there

> *fell* instead of *feel*
>> *pass* instead of *past; heave* instead of *heavy*

What are you like instead of *What do you like*

> *I fell so hurt that all you made for me, they took*

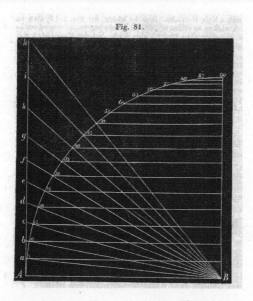

Fig. 81.

How to leak a starling from the mouth; tear the air. How to loosen threads enough to twine in, how to keep stray ends under the tongue. How to steep a worn texture, which is to say familiar, of family, *mine.* How to steep translucence. How to know, not know, it was like this all along. How to, say, *not* call myself to others, but draw the world around me. According to *my* sound. How to say, *This is, This is, This is.*

How to Build an American Home

A home is a hemispherical world.
Say interior of equatorial house.
Say slice-cut of X, say wing-turn of Y. Say it lateral and broken
and call it right.

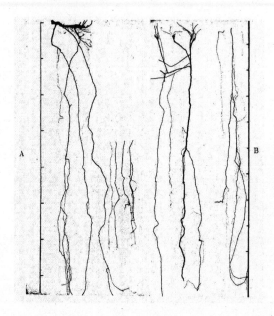

In other words: Find a blueprint, submerge it in water. Or, hold
    your tracing paper to the crack in the ceiling.

      X is where we rename the grid until its lines are all off-center
                 loosening
                      into shorelines impossible
to say. X: beginning at my throat,
beginning in numerical allusions, and soon we are inside
                    a blurred circumference,
      a mirror with more than one anchor.

How to Build an American Home

1: your language of intimacy and the slant of afternoon stratosphere 2: the study of how species space themselves with respect to one another 3: if sound had a surface, if language measured distance, if the body was a metaphor for everything unsaid 4: *home-based sense of identity 5: interacting with intimates 6: fossilization*, one's language cut transversely and encased in time and atmosphere 7: when I listen to someone speak, the vibration of my own body 8: *bone language*.

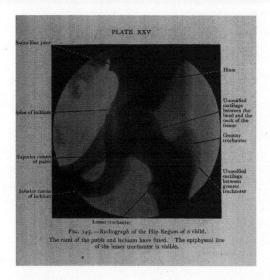

On their way to the ancestral graves:

                                    it was on an island
and she was not quite sure how to reach it. If a cargo boat passes by in bright
yellow and reddened paint, then a sound will occur in her heart like a massive
train crossing a bridge overhead.

How to Build an American Home

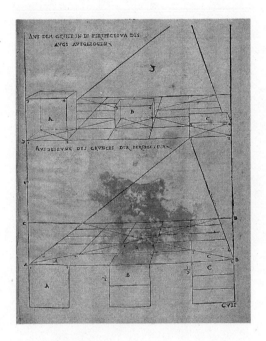

If there is a word for *to gleam through soot* and another for *smoke-black*, then somewhere also is
> *dust, fume, dim,*
which would mean flying dust or bright smoke.

                We will always hold those who kept us in the world before we could fall out again. Geometry is a configuration of parts, each asking itself: *How do I adhere?* It is a tricky matter: in order to unfold a multi-sided structure under a plain sky, we must draw on murky shifts that crack and tumble in the underground.

How to Build an American Home

Strata is what you call rock that has been compressed over time.
To unrest its layers, to breaker

                              an opening
        we might locate
        a crevice,
                count our way down,
                              leaving the silences in place,
                          keeping the splinters for ourselves.

Strata is what exists;
Strata is what layers and shifts according to our very existence.

How to Build an American Home

Whereas sound opens up the space behind us, which we cannot see.
Whereas sound is the distance between two ghosts, the effect of two surfaces
rubbing against each other.

What, then, is the sound I make
to say, *here?*

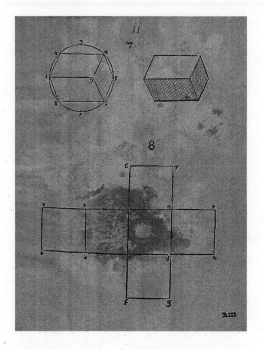

        Foreign matter creeps into her father's speech,
something that bleeds in a sink full of water;

        When the voice begins to seep inside the house,
then she knows the framework is full of defects: insect holes along the
backyard base, creatures swimming in the attic veins, mold-ridden cracks
that continue to deepen like crusty fingernails after she has gone to bed.

How to Build an American Home

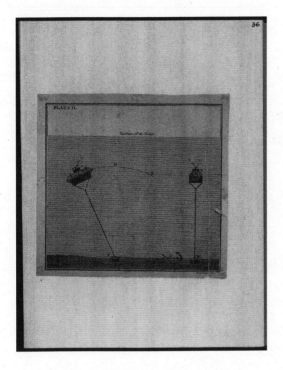

heisenberg uncertainty principle:

No one told me how to mark the gaps between us, how to
compensate for them in the first place.

> No one told me that if I left, there would always
> be a reason to return.

How to Build an American Home

      When the father reminds her to exercise the eyes by staring at the horizon, it is a lesson in distance.
          As if he knew how the distance to an object is felt as
                              the distance to one's body.

Inside the house of his birth years, she unlocked
the door, and amidst the dust of translucent curtain, wooden washboard,
overgrown courtyard, cabinet of forgotten vanquishings, she saw all she could
        have was the nearness of the faraway hour between stale walls.

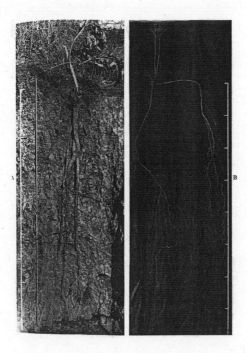

to create a long narrow opening by cracking or splitting rock : to forge a breakage in known structures without even knowing : to breach, rupture, shift, disrupt : to crawl down and sleep : a schism or groove we can then grow through : akin to *a deep division between parts of the body*, as in *cloven,* as in *we cleave* : children of immigrants speak in earthquakes : gaps, fissures, intervals.

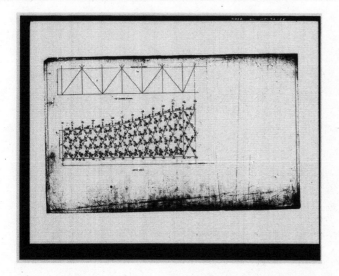

A house reflects its weathering.

We count the ways in which we burrow, given the atmosphere.

In the distance a fine hairline of trees are measuring themselves
against a dark cloud above.

How to Build an American Home

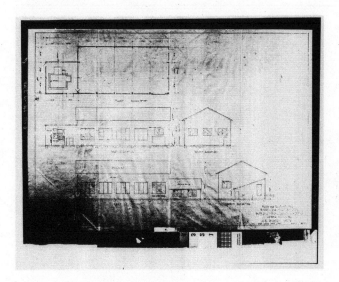

      For there was a night where I slept
deeply, and had heavy nightmares:

                        a dark house that I must lock
           from the back,
               a house I must leave
        before forgotten shapes return.

How to Build an American Home

When they leave the house,
she will place her arm between the light
to still her mother in shadow. As if her body
could approximate the house.

To love a mother: to forfeit sounds from the mouth: to catch
instead a body's sideswept pitch: to hold her there.

How to Build an American Home

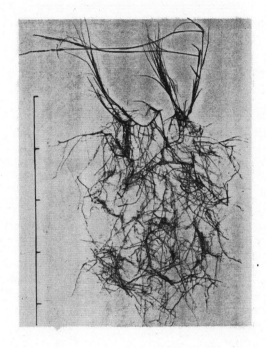

                    to stake the water:
to keep it safe: to nest
        against all weathers: to nest the swell—

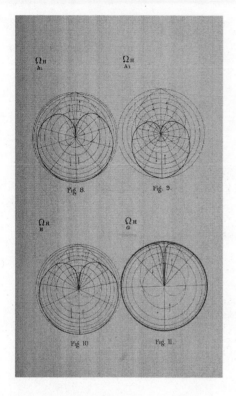

If the body is
    a gathering of reverberations and tides;

        the smallest angle at which I turn away
     while you are pointed at the sun

If belonging is not a figment of the mind but
          an attunement of earth and breaks—

How to Build an American Home

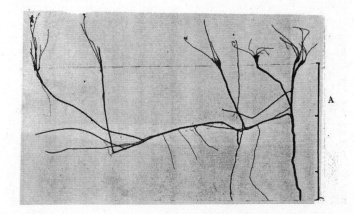

A family does its fieldwork in the undersides.
She played beneath the kitchen table imagining its legs as the ribcage
of a whale.

Keep the stock full. Stay your head even. Hold the loose ends.

Pressed against the colossal heartbeat: a warm thunder.

Held between two skeins, the air becomes a cradle.

A grid is something that grows with the terrain. We mine for the textures we can. Cut this ocean in half, a cross-section of water; watch this shadow alight from this angle in the dark. To bind this house with wounded thread. To cast it into the hearth of a sky.

How to Build an American Home

To prevent an invasion of overhead winds, I placed my child heart near the skin of the floor and wafted in a condensation of history. I drew up neat boundaries of *here* and *there*, *we* and *they*, and held my arms open to the walls. A lungful of door hinge, thumbprint of the window seam. A house steeps in spoonfuls of patterns, ghosts, leaves. Children of immigrants gather bits of wire, thread, a safety pin; they arrange them like a blueprint, not knowing why or how they know the shape.

How to Build an American Home

Rather than reorienting toward spatial geometries, new geographies,
the body is a plane that has already been inscribed. Newspaper stories of
bodies bent over, bodies in shame, a continuation of angles yet to be
unlearned. If we could trace such a system of invisible dimensions, unearth
an inheritance of fractures and cracks, we would know once and for all how
decades have no margins, oceans do not stop.

Notes

Quotations in *Letters to Mao* are from the following sources:

> P. 16: Terms and phrases in italics are from Giulio Tononi, "Sleep and Dreaming," *The Neurology of Consciousness* (Academic Press, 2008).
>
> P. 54: *"archaeology of ritualized movement"* is from Paul Garwood, "Rites of Passage," *The Oxford Handbook of the Archaeology of Ritual and Religion*, ed. Timothy Insoll (Oxford University Press, 2012).

Definitions of terms in *House A; Geometry B* draw on language from the *New Oxford American Dictionary*. Additional language and quotations are from various sources:

> C: "here we participate in the carpenter's solid geometry" and "a house constitutes a body of images" are from Gaston Bachelard, *Poetics of Space* (Beacon Press, 1994).
>
> D: *"diagram of the functions of inhabiting"* is from Gaston Bachelard, *Poetics of Space* (Beacon Press, 1994).
>
> F: "not in the thing itself but in the patterns of shadows" is from Junichiro Tanizaki, *In Praise of Shadows* (Leete's Island Books, 1977).
>
> G: "a *no place, a nowhere*, an imaginary space longed for" is from Susan Stanford Friedman, quoted in Lisa Knopp, *The Nature of Home: A Lexicon and Essays* (Bison Books, 2004).
>
> G: The underlying language in *"an unfinished place of historical and geographical boundaries"* is from Carol Bigwood, quoted in Lisa Knopp, *The Nature of Home: A Lexicon and Essays* (Bison Books, 2004).
>
> O: "and when the seeping starts, the house is already completed" is from Gaston Bachelard, *Poetics of Space* (Beacon Press, 1994).
>
> T: The underlying quotation for "identify and measure the [acoustic intervals] of global migration, settlement... histories and historiography" is from "Global Mixed Race" (conference abstract for Critical Mixed Race Studies, DePaul University, Chicago, IL, 2014).
>
> X: *"i have roots that are most [secret], i am grown in the deep earth"* is from Sigmund Freud, "The 'Uncanny'" (1919).
>
> Z: The underlying quotation for "possible [metrics]: contact zone, borderlands. language in construction of multiple histories" is from "Language Speaks Us" (conference abstract, College English Association at the University of Puerto Rico at Mayaguez, Puerto Rico, 2014).

Images in *How to Build an American Home* are from the following sources (in public domain):

P. 79: "Parachutes open overhead," 1944, National Archives and Records Administration.

P. 80: Nehemiah Grew, *The Comparative Anatomy of Trunks*, 1675. Digital copy by Paul K is licensed under CC BY 2.0. https://creativecommons.org/licenses/by/2.0/

P. 81: "Moon Model Prepared by Johann Friedrich Julius Schmidt," 1898, Field Museum Library / Getty Images.

P. 82: "Transit of Venus," 1882, United States Naval Observatory.

P. 83, 99, 102: Augustin Hirschvogel, Geometria, 1543.

P. 84: Nehemiah Grew, *An Idea of a Phytological History Propounded, Together with a Continuation of the Anatomy of Vegetables, Particularly Prosecuted upon Roots*, 1673. Digital copy by Paul K is licensed under CC BY 2.0. https://creativecommons.org/licenses/by/2.0/

P. 85: Hendrik van Reede tot Drakestein, *Hortus Indicus Malabaricus*, Vol 3, 1678-1693.

P. 86, 96, 105, 109, 111: John E. Weaver, *The ecological relation of roots*, 1919, Library of Congress.

P. 87: Percival Lowell, *Mars*, 1896.

P. 88, 90, 110: Louisa S. Cook, *Geometrical Psychology*, 1887.

P. 89: John P. Soule, "Skeleton Leaves," c.1871-1879, Library of Congress.

P. 91: *The Intellectual observer*, 1862-1868.

P. 92: "Hun T'ien Yi T'ung Hsing Hsiang Ch'uan T'u," c.1600. Image courtesy Adler Planetarium, Chicago, IL.

P. 93: Anna Atkins, "Laminaria bulbosa," 1843-1853, New York Public Library.

P. 94: Anton Steinhauser, "Grundzüge der mathematischen Geographie…," 1857, The British Library.

P. 95: "observatory 01429," 1874/1882, U.S. Naval Observatory.

P. 97: Anna Atkins, "Gelidium corneum vars", 1843-1853, New York Public Library.

P. 98: Arthur Robinson, *Cunningham's Manual of Practical Anatomy*, 7th ed, 1920.

P. 100: West Coast Art Co, "Sierra Nevada Mts," c.1911, Library of Congress.

P. 101: West Coast Art Co, "Salt River Valley," 1913, Library of Congress.

P. 103: Alexander Anderson, "[Diagram for underwater apparatus]," 1775-1870, Print Collection, Miriam and Ira D. Wallach Division of Art, Prints and Photographs, The New York Public Library, Astor,

Lenox and Tilden Foundations.

P. 104: "9. Photocopy of blueprint…," Library of Congress.

P. 106: "55. Draw Span Truss Geometry…," Library of Congress.

P. 107: "10. Photocopy of architectural blueprint..," Library of Congress.

P. 108: American Colony (Jerusalem), Photo Dept, "Geology. Petrified bird's nest," 1920-1933, Library of Congress.

P. 112: Thomas Hibben, "Detail of rammed earth," 1937, Library of Congress.

P. 113: "18. Photocopy of aerial photograph…," 1895, Library of Congress.

P. 114: "[Otto Lilienthal gliding experiment]," [1895?], Library of Congress.

Quotations in *How to Build an American Home* are from the following sources:

P. 81: "*coexistence between one's body and an inhabited surface*" is from Setha M. Low, "Embodied Space(s): Anthropological Theories of Body, Space, and Culture," *Space and Culture*, 6: 9, 2003.

P. 82: "*semantic template*" is from Katharine Young, "Touch: The Common Sense" (class lecture, Anthropology of the Body, San Francisco State University, San Francisco, CA, Spring 2014).

P. 91: "*embodied spaces*" is from Setha M. Low, "Embodied Space(s): Anthropological Theories of Body, Space, and Culture," Space and Culture, 6: 9, 2003.

P. 95: "*interior of equatorial house*" is the caption for another photograph of the same structure depicted in the image, from the U.S. Naval Observatory.

P. 97: "*home-based sense of identity*" and "*interacting with intimates*" are from James Gee, "Literacy, Discourse, and Linguistics," *Journal of Education*, 171: 1, 1989.

P. 105: The language in this poem is based on the dictionary definitions and synonyms for *fissure*.

Acknowledgments

This book contains layers of gratitude. Most heartfelt to Claudia Rankine for seeing something in my manuscript, and to the editors at Omnidawn, especially Rusty Morrison and Gillian Olivia Blythe Hamel, for the attention and energy poured into this object.

I am grateful to the editors of the journals in which versions of these poems appeared—*Web Conjunctions*, *Mid-American Review*, *Tin House*, *Tarpaulin Sky*, *Ninth Letter*, *DIAGRAM*, *Cherry Tree*, *Columbia Poetry Review*, *New American Writing*, and *Dusie*; to Richard Garcia for choosing one of my *Letters to Mao* as winner of the *Mid-American Review* Fineline Prize; to the Academy of American Poets for the Harold Taylor Award; and to the creative writing department at San Francisco State University for the Ann Fields Poetry Prize.

At the beginning was Catherine Imbriglio, who showed me a language in which my voice could exist.

I am grateful to Barbara Tomash for her generosity of support, insight, and magic; to my classmates who read parts of my manuscript; to the SFSU CW community and faculty, especially Maxine Chernoff, Toni Mirosevich, and Truong Tran; to my Drop Leaf Press sisters; and to the love song that is my Kundiman family.

This first book was emboldened by many who provided strength and confidence in various ways: Arya Asemanfar, Donna Chan, April Freely, Sarah Heady, David Hill, Tiffanie Hoang, Tanya Holtland, Ahran Lee, Selina Lai, Jessica Lian, Jackie Jia Lou, Henry Leung, Adam Manfredi, Susan Naylor, Ploi Pirapokin, Keane Shum, Rohith Ravi, Neetu Rohith, Raul Ruiz, Maude Tanswai, Christina Tran, Spring Ulmer, Heidi Van Horn, Xu Xi, and my lifelong kindred souls Angela Pan Wong and Grace You.

Thank you to my family for my deepest sense of home and for being supportive even when you did not fully understand; to my in-laws for your open hearts; to my grandparents, aunts, and uncles, whose stories are shrouded but whom I love profoundly; to my brother who will hold my hand if I ask for it, to my sister who is my biggest fan, and to my parents who worked hard all your lives so I could have choices you never had.

Thank you, from depths and depths, to my loved one, Gary Tsang, for encouraging me on unfamiliar paths, for being there in every tangible and intangible way, and for exploring this world, its holes and its beauties, and making a place in it with me.

And you, Invisible House.

Jennifer S. Cheng is a poet and essayist with MFA degrees from the University of Iowa and San Francisco State University and a BA from Brown University. A US Fulbright scholar, Kundiman fellow, and Pushcart Prize nominee, she is the author of an image-text chapbook, *Invocation: An Essay* (New Michigan Press), and her writing appears in *Tin House*, *AGNI*, *Mid-American Review*, *DIAGRAM*, *Tarpaulin Sky*, *The Volta* and elsewhere. Having grown up in Texas, Hong Kong, and Connecticut, she currently lives in San Francisco. www.jenniferscheng.com.

House A
Jennifer S. Cheng

Cover photograph by Mitsu Yoshikawa.
www.mitsuyoshikawa-image.com

Cover and interior text set in Optima LT Std and Adobe Garamond Pro

Cover and interior design by Gillian Olivia Blythe Hamel

Printed in the United States
by Books International, Dulles, Virginia
On 55# Glatfelter B19 Antique
Acid Free Archival Quality Recycled Paper

Publication of this book was made possible in part by gifts from:
The New Place Fund
Robin & Curt Caton

Omnidawn Publishing
Oakland, California
2016

Rusty Morrison & Ken Keegan, senior editors & co-publishers
Gillian Olivia Blythe Hamel, managing editor
Cassandra Smith, poetry editor & book designer
Peter Burghardt, poetry editor
Sharon Zetter, poetry editor, book designer & development officer
Liza Flum, poetry editor & marketing assistant
Juliana Paslay, fiction editor
Gail Aronson, fiction editor
Kevin Peters, marketing assistant & OmniVerse Lit Scene editor
Cameron Stuart, marketing assistant
Sara Burant, administrative assistant
Avren Keating, administrative assistant
Josie Gallup, publicity assistant
SD Sumner, copyeditor